A SNOWBOARD SHOW

Julie Moriarty

ISBN 0-439-74473-3

SCHOLASTIC, SCHOLASTIC FX BOOKS, and associated logos and designs are trademarks and/or registered trademarks of Scholastic Inc.

LEXILE is a registered trademark of MetaMetrics, Inc.

5   6   7   8   9   10   23   14 13 12 11 10

SCHOLASTIC INC.

New York   Toronto   London   Auckland   Sydney
Mexico City   New Delhi   Hong Kong   Buenos Aires

SNOWBOARD WORDS

Check out these words before you read. Then look for them in the book.

Bowl: The bottom of a halfpipe. (See photo.)

Catch air: To ride high in the air on a snowboard.

Halfpipe: The spot in the snow where boarders do tricks. It looks like the bottom half of a tunnel. (See photo.)

Bowl

Lip

Halfpipe

Lip: The top edge of one side of a halfpipe. (See photo.)

McTwist: A snowboard trick. You spin and flip at the same time.

Shred: To mess up the snow. (That's a good thing!)

Shut the window!

It's cold and you feel frozen.

There is so much snow! I know, let's go to

a snowboard show.

First, here's something you should know. Don't try the tricks in this book. These boarders are trained pros.

Let it rip! <u>Soko</u> drops into the **b o w l.** Then pop! She catches air. <u>Soko</u> is seven feet up!

The kids <u>below</u> grin. "<u>Go</u>, <u>Soko</u>!" they <u>bellow</u>.

<u>Soko Yamaoka</u>

4

Tommy gets to the lip of the halfpipe. Then it's time to focus. Tommy jumps. He catches air. Over he goes!

Tommy Czeschin

Tommy knows his stuff. "And I have a lot of fun doing it," he says. He shreds the snow, and the others follow.

Kelly <u>coasts</u> along the **halfpipe.** She has <u>grown</u> up on a snowboard. She makes it look <u>so</u> simple. But it's not! <u>Whoa</u>! Kelly wins a <u>gold</u>!

Kelly Clark

Kier Dillon

Kier is not <u>slow</u> on his board. Today, he <u>shows</u> off the **McTwist**.

He tucks his <u>elbows</u> and bends <u>low</u>. His hands <u>hold</u> the board. Will he <u>blow</u> it? <u>No</u>! His trick <u>goes</u> well. In fact, he scores <u>bonus</u> points!

Torah lands all of her runs. She rides fast as she hits the ramp. Her <u>coach</u> is happy. <u>So</u> is Torah. She <u>glows</u> after the <u>show</u>.

Torah Jones Bright